LITTLE CINDERELLA

A Picture Book

JULIA JOHNS

[ZHINGOORA BOOKS]

LITTLE CINDERELLA.

4

In former times, a rich man and his wife were the parents of a beautiful little daughter; but before she had arrived at womanhood, her dear mother fell sick, and seeing that death was near, she called her little child to her, and thus addressed her: "My child, always be good, and bear everything that occurs to you with patience; then, whatever toil and troubles you may suffer during life, happiness will be your lot in the end."

After uttering these words the poor lady died, and her daughter was overwhelmed with grief at the loss of so good and kind a mother.

The father, too, was very unhappy; but he sought to get rid of his sorrow by marrying another wife; and he looked for some amiable lady who might be a second mother to his child, and a companion to himself. Unfortunately, his choice fell on a widow lady, of a proud and overbearing temper, who had two daughters by a former marriage, both as haughty and bad-tempered as herself.

Before marriage this woman had the cunning to conceal her bad qualities so well that she appeared to be very amiable; but the marriage was scarcely over when her real character showed itself. She could not endure her amiable step-daughter, with all her charming qualifications; for they only made her own daughters appear more hateful. She gave her the most degrading occupations, and compelled her to wash the dishes and clean the stairs, and to sweep her own rooms and those of her sisters-in-law

When the poor girl had finished her work, she used
to sit in the 8chimney-corner amongst the cinders,
which made her sisters give her the name of
"Cinderella." However, in her shabby clothes
Cinderella was ten times handsomer than her
sisters, let them be ever so magnificently dressed.

The poor girl slept in the garret, upon a wretched straw mattress, whilst the bed-chambers of her sisters were furnished with every luxury and elegance, and provided with mirrors, in which they could survey themselves from head to foot. The amiable creature bore this ill treatment with patience, and did not venture to complain to her father, who was so completely governed by his wife that he would only have scolded her.

It happened that the king's son sent invitations to a ball, which was to last two nights, and to which all the great people of the land were invited, the two sisters among the rest. This delighted them extremely, and their thoughts were entirely occupied in selecting their most becoming dresses for the important occasion. Poor Cinderella had now more work to do than ever, as it was her business to iron their linen, and starch their ruffles. The sisters talked of nothing but preparations for the ball. The eldest said, "I shall wear my crimson-velvet dress, and point-lace;" and the younger, "I shall put on my usual dress-petticoat, a mantle embroidered with gold flowers, and a tiara of diamonds." They sent to engage the services of the most fashionable hairdresser. They also called Cinderella to their aid; for she had very good taste, and she offered, in the most amiable manner, to arrange their heads herself; of which offer they were only too happy to avail themselves.

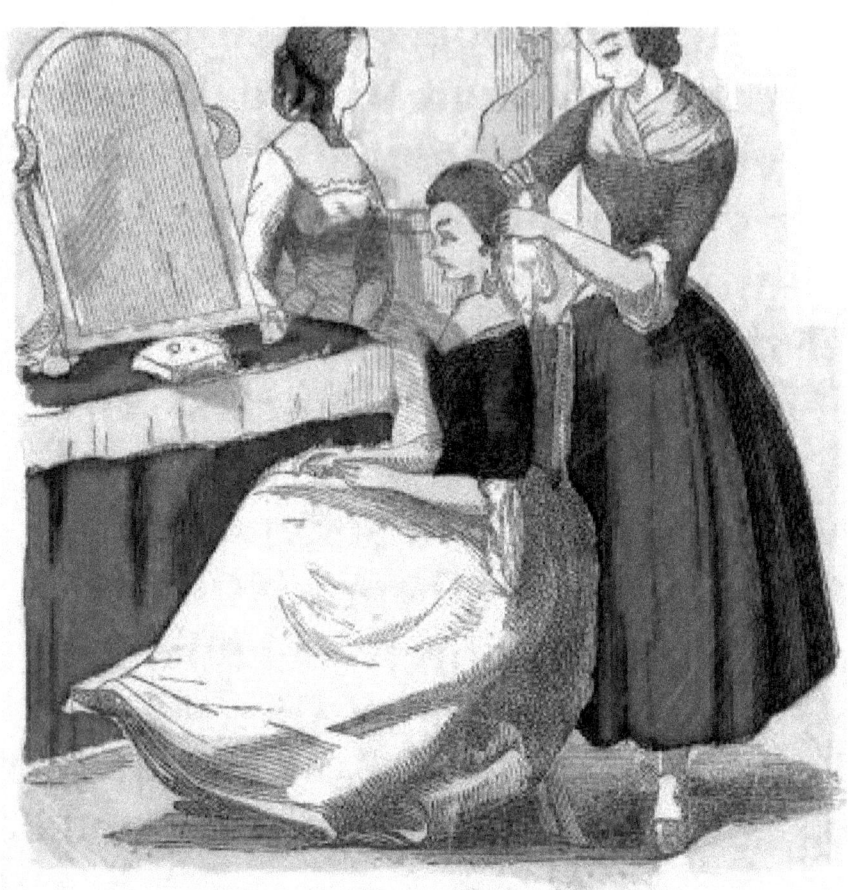

Whilst so occupied, the eldest said, "Cinderella, should you like to go to the ball?"

"Alas!" said she, "you are ridiculing me. I am not likely to go to the ball."

"You are right," replied the sister; "people would be amused to see a Cinderella there."

If Cinderella had been at all unamiable she might have dressed their heads all awry, for such unkindness; but she returned good for evil, and did it in the best possible style.

The sisters were in such spirits they could scarcely eat for two days. All their time was spent before the looking-glass, and more than a dozen laces were broken in attempts to tighten their waists into elegant shapes.

At length the long-wished-for evening arrived, and these proud misses stepped into their carriage, and drove away to the palace.

Cinderella looked after the coach as far as she could see, and then returned to the kitchen in tears, where, for the first time, she bewailed her hard and cruel lot, little dreaming that a kind fairy was at the same moment watching over her.

She continued sobbing in the chimney-corner
until a rap at the door aroused her, and she got up
to see what had caused it. She found a little old
woman, hobbling on crutches, who besought her to
give her some food.

"I have only part of my own supper for you, Goody,
which is no better than a dry crust. But if you will
step in and warm yourself by the fire, you can do
so, and welcome."

"Thank you, my dear," said the old woman, in a
feeble, croaking voice; and when she had hobbled in,
and taken her seat by the fire, she continued, "Hey!
dearee me! what are all these tears about, my child?"

And then Cinderella told her of all her griefs,—how
her sisters had gone to the ball, and how she should
like to have gone also.

"But you shall go,„ exclaimed her visitor, who was suddenly transformed into a beautiful fairy, "or I am not queen of the fairies, or your godmother. Dry up your tears, my dear goddaughter, and do as I bid you, and you shall have clothes and horses finer than any one."

As Cinderella had often heard her father talk of her godmother, and tell her that she was one of those kind fairies who protect good children, her spirits revived, and she wiped away her tears.

The fairy took Cinderella by the hand, and said, "Now, my dear, go into the garden, and fetch me a pumpkin."

Cinderella went immediately to gather the best she could find, and carried it to her godmother, though she could not guess how this pumpkin could make her go to the ball. Her godmother took the pumpkin and hollowed it out, leaving only the rind; she then struck it with her wand, and the pumpkin was immediately changed into a beautiful gilt coach. She next sent Cinderella for the mouse-trap, wherein were found six mice alive. She directed Cinderella to raise the door of the trap, and as each mouse came out she struck it with her wand, and it was immediately changed into a beautiful horse; so that she had now six splendid grays for her gilt coach.

The fairy was perplexed how to find a coachman, but Cinderella said, "I will go and see if there is a rat in the rat-trap; if there is, he will make a capital coachman."

"You are right," said the godmother; "go and see." Cinderella brought the rat-trap, in which there were three large rats. The fairy selected one, on account of its beautiful whiskers, and, having touched it, it was changed into a fat coachman, with the finest pair of whiskers that ever were seen. She then said, "You must now go into the garden, where you will find six lizards, behind the watering-pot; bring them to me." These were no sooner brought than the godmother changed them into six tall footmen, in handsome liveries, with cocked hats and gold-headed canes, who jumped up behind the coach just as if they had been accustomed to it all their lives.16

The coachman and postilion having likewise taken their places, the fairy said to Cinderella, "Well, my dear girl, is not this as fine an equipage as you could desire, to go to the ball with? Tell me, now, are you pleased with it?"

"O yes, dear godmother," replied Cinderella; and then, with a good deal of hesitation, she added, "but how can I make my appearance among so many finely-dressed people in these shabby clothes?"

"Give yourself no uneasiness about that, my dear. The most difficult part of our task is already accomplished, and it will be hard if I cannot make your dress correspond with your coach and servants."

On saying this, the fairy touched Cinderella with her magic wand, and her clothes were instantly changed into a most magnificent ball-dress, ornamented with the most costly

jewels. The
fairy now took from her pocket a beautiful pair of
elastic glass slippers, which17 she caused
Cinderella to put on; and when she had thus
completed her work, and Cinderella stood before her,
arrayed in her beautiful clothes, the fairy was
much pleased, and desired her to get into the
carriage with all expedition, as the ball had already
commenced. Two of the footmen then sprang and
opened the carriage-door, and assisted Cinderella
into it. Her godmother, however, before she took
leave, strictly charged her on no account whatever
to stay at the ball after the clock had struck the
hour of midnight; and then added that if she
stopped but a single moment beyond that time her
fine coach would again become a gourd, her horses

mice, her footmen lizards, and her old clothes resume their former appearance.

Cinderella promised faithfully to attend to everything that the fairy had mentioned; and then, quite overjoyed, gave the direction to the footman, who bawled out, in a loud voice, to the coachman, "To the royal palace!"

The coachman touched his prancing horses lightly with his whip, and swiftly the carriage started off, and in a short time reached the palace.

The arrival of so splendid an equipage as Cinderella's could not fail to attract general notice at the palace gates, and as it drove up to the marble portico the servants, in great numbers, came out to see it.

The king's son, to whom it was announced that an unknown princess had arrived, hastened to receive her. He handed her out of the carriage, and led her to the ball-room. Immediately she entered the dancing ceased, and the violins stopped playing; so much was every one struck with the extreme beauty of the unknown princess; and the only sound heard was that of admiration. The king, old as he was, could not take his eyes off her, and said, in a low voice to the queen, that he had not seen such a beautiful person for many years. All the ladies began examining her dress, that they might have similar ones the next evening, if it was possible to obtain equally rich stuffs, and work-people skilled enough to make them. The king's son conducted her to the most distinguished place, and invited her to dance. She danced with such grace that everybody was in raptures with her; and when supper was served the prince could partake of nothing, so much was he occupied in contemplating the beauty of the fair stranger.

Seated close to her sisters, Cinderella showed them marked attention, and divided with them the oranges and citrons which the prince had given her; all of which surprised them greatly, as they did not recognize her.

When Cinderella saw that it wanted but a quarter of an hour of midnight she left as quickly as possible, making a low courtesy to all the company.

On reaching home she found her godmother there, thanked her for the delightful evening she had spent, and begged permission to go to the ball the following night, as the prince had desired her company. The fairy kindly granted her request, on condition that she would return before twelve. She then caused her clothes to resume their usual plainness, that her sisters might not know of her adventure.

Whilst Cinderella was occupied in relating all that had passed at the ball to her godmother, the two sisters knocked at the door, and as she went to open it for them the fairy disappeared.

"O, how late you are in coming home," said Cinderella, rubbing her eyes, as if just awakened.

"If you had been at the ball," said one of the sisters, "you would not have been tired; for there was there the most beautiful princess that ever was seen, who paid us much attention, and gave us oranges and citrons."

Cinderella could scarcely contain herself for joy. She asked the name of the princess, but they said it was not known, and that the king's son was therefore much distressed, and would give anything he had to know who she could be.

Cinderella smiled, and said, "Was she, then, so very beautiful? Could not I see her? O, Javotte, do lend me your yellow dress, that you wear every day, that I may go to the ball, and have a peep at this wonderful princess!"

"Indeed," said Javotte, "I am not so silly as to lend my dress to a wretched Cinderella like you."

Cinderella expected this refusal, and was very glad of it; for she would have been greatly embarrassed if her sister had lent her the dress.

The next evening the sisters again went to the ball, and Cinderella soon made her appearance, more magnificently dressed than before. The king's son was constantly at her side, saying the most agreeable things; so that Cinderella did not notice how the time passed, and had quite forgot her godmother's injunctions. While she therefore thought it was scarcely eleven o'clock, she was startled by the first stroke of midnight. She rose very hastily, and fled as lightly as a fawn, the prince following, though he could not overtake her. In her flight she let one of her glass slippers fall, which the prince picked up with the greatest care.

Cinderella arrived at home out of breath, without carriage or servants, in her shabby clothes, and had nothing remaining of all her former magnificence except one of her little glass slippers,—the fellow of that she had lost.

Upon inquiry being made of the guards, at the palace gates, as to whether the princess had gone out, they replied that they had seen no one go out but a young girl, very poorly dressed, who looked more like a peasant than a fine lady.

When the two sisters returned from the ball Cinderella asked if they had enjoyed themselves, and if the beautiful lady had again been there. They told her that she had been there, but that when the clock struck twelve she had started off so quickly that she let one of her pretty glass slippers fall off; that the prince, who quickly followed her, had picked it up, and had done nothing but look at it all the rest of the evening; and that he was evidently very much in love with the beautiful creature to whom it belonged, and would spare no pains to find her.

This was indeed the case; for, a few days after, the prince caused it to be published, with the sound of trumpets, that he would marry the lady whose foot would exactly fit the slipper.

So the slipper was first tried on by all the princesses, then by all the duchesses, and next by all the ladies belonging to the court; but in vain. It was then taken to the two sisters, who tried every possible way of getting their foot into it, but without success.

Cinderella, who was looking at them, and now recognized her slipper, said, laughingly, "Let me see if it will fit me."

The sisters immediately began to laugh, and to ridicule her; but the gentleman who had been appointed to try on the slipper, having looked attentively at Cinderella, and finding her very pretty, said she was quite right in her request; for he was ordered to try it on to everybody.

He desired her to sit down, and at once found that the slipper would go on her foot, without any trouble, and, indeed, fitted her like wax.

The astonishment of the sisters was very great, but still greater when Cinderella drew from her pocket the fellow-slipper, and, to the great delight of the gentleman, placed it upon her other foot.

Her godmother now made her appearance, and, having touched Cinderella with her wand, she made her look even more magnificent than on either of the former occasions.

The sisters now recognized in Cinderella the beautiful person they had seen at the ball, and threw themselves at her feet, to implore forgiveness for all the ill-treatment they had shown her. Cinderella raised them up, and, embracing them, said she forgave them, with all her heart, their unkindness to her, and hoped that for the future they would be more kind in their behavior to every one about them. She told them she had never forgotten the last words of her mother, on her death-bed:—"My child, always be good, and bear with patience everything that occurs to you; then, whatever toils and troubles you may suffer during life, happiness will be your lot in the end."

These words now proved to be true; for, having borne unkindness and cruelty with patience ever since her father's second marriage, she was now going to be the wife of the king's son.

Cinderella then explained the visit of her godmother, the queen of the fairies; and how her magic wand had furnished her with dresses, carriages, and attendants; and how, by forgetting the good fairy's orders, she was obliged to quit the ball-room so suddenly; and how, in her haste, she lost her little glass slipper, and, for her disobedience, was deprived of all her fine clothes.

Cinderella being now betrothed to the prince, she was taken to the palace, dressed in all her splendor; and, being as amiable as she was beautiful, invited her sisters to live in the palace with her, where they were soon married to two great lords belonging to the court.

The prince thought Cinderella more beautiful than ever, and in a few days married her. She was most happy in the love of her husband, the esteem of the court, and the good-will of all who knew her.

End of the book.